A Christmas Musical for Two-Part Choir

by Richard Kingsmore and Christopher Machen

Copyright © 1996 by Pilot Point Music.
All rights reserved. Litho in U.S.A.

KANSAS CITY, MO 64141

CONTENTS

FOR UNTO US 3
    For unto Us
    Joy to the World
    Angels We Have Heard on High

NARRATION 1 13

LIGHT OF THE WORLD 14
    with O Come, All Ye Faithful

WORSHIP THE KING 25

CHRISTMAS MEMORIES (Vignette) 35

CHRISTMAS MEMORIES (Underscore) 36

NARRATION 2 37

WONDERFUL COUNSELOR 38

THE LETTER (Vignette) 47

THE LETTER (Underscore) 48

NARRATION 3 49

MIGHTY GOD 50

PRINCE OF PEACE 61
    with Silent Night

THE WISH (Vignette) 64

NARRATION 4 70

EVERLASTING FATHER 71

BORN IS THE KING 78
    The First Noel
    Hark! the Herald Angels Sing
    The Birthday of a King

NARRATION 5 86

THE NAME OF JESUS 87
    with For unto Us

Copyright © 1996 by Pilot Point Music. All rights reserved.
Administered by The Copyright Company, 40 Music Square East, Nashville, TN 37203.

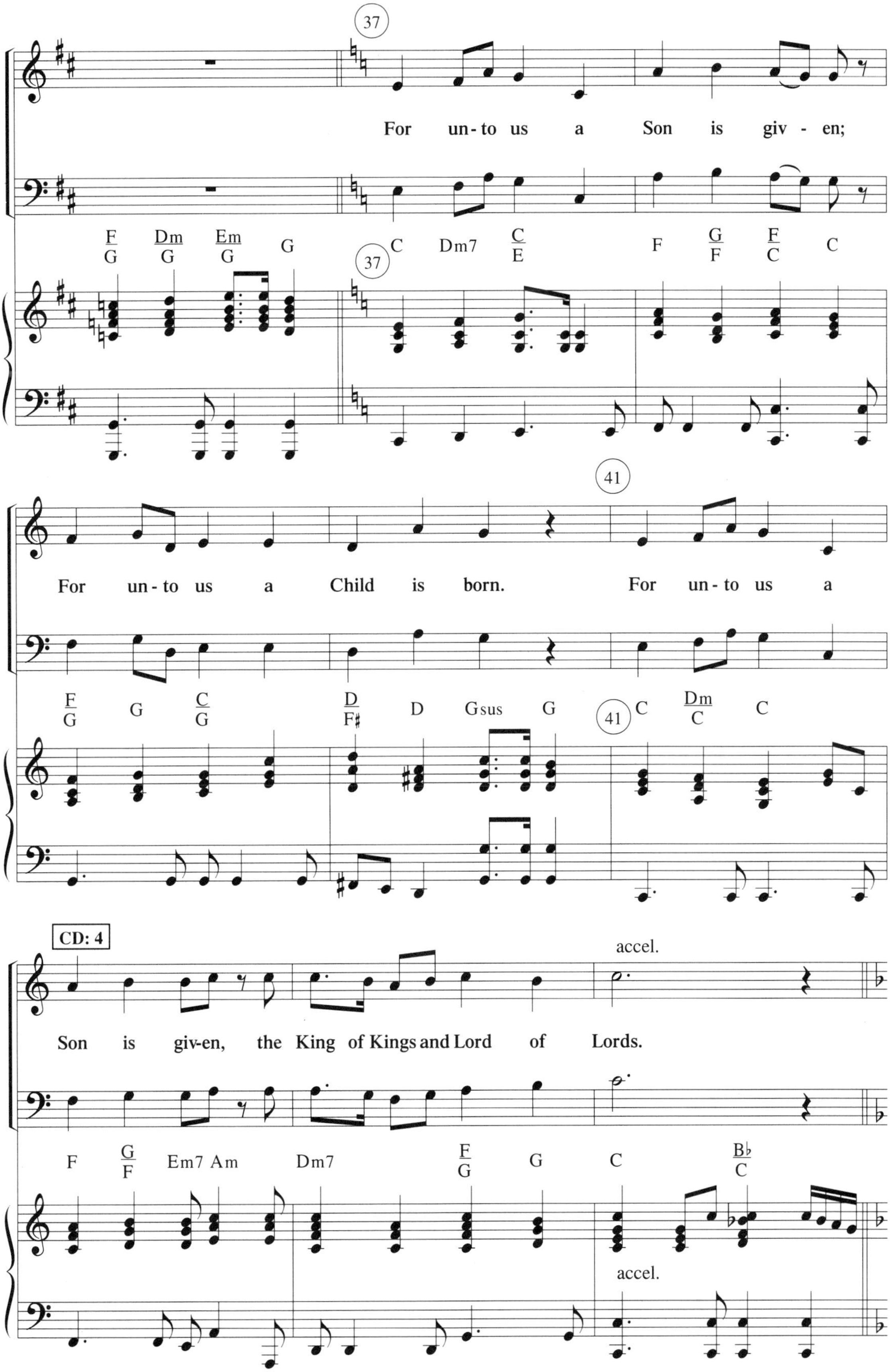
37
For un-to us a Son is giv - en;
F/G Dm/G Em/G G C Dm7 C/E F G/F F/C C
For un-to us a Child is born. For un-to us a
41
F/G G C/G D/F♯ D Gsus G C Dm/C C
CD: 4
accel.
Son is giv-en, the King of Kings and Lord of Lords.
F G/F Em7 Am Dm7 F/G G C B♭/C
accel.

Narration 1

"For unto us a Child is born, unto us a Son is given. And the government shall be upon His shoulder, and His name shall be called Wonderful Counselor, the Mighty God, the Everlasting Father, the Prince of Peace." Jesus was known by many names. Each name reveals the immensity of God's love for His children. In Jesus' name we find hope for the future and peace for our present lives. Just the sound of His name dispels the darkness of this world and fills it with radiant light.

Light of the World

with
O Come, All Ye Faithful

Words and Music by
CHRISTOPHER MACHEN
Arr. by Richard Kingsmore

Copyright © 1996 by Pilot Point Music. All rights reserved.
Administered by The Copyright Company, 40 Music Square East, Nashville, TN 37203.
*Arr. © 1996 by Pilot Point Music. All rights reserved. Administered by The Copyright Company, 40 Music Square East, Nashville, TN 37203.

In Jesus' name we find hope for the future and peace for our present lives. Just the sound of His name dispells the darkness of this world and fills it with radiant light.

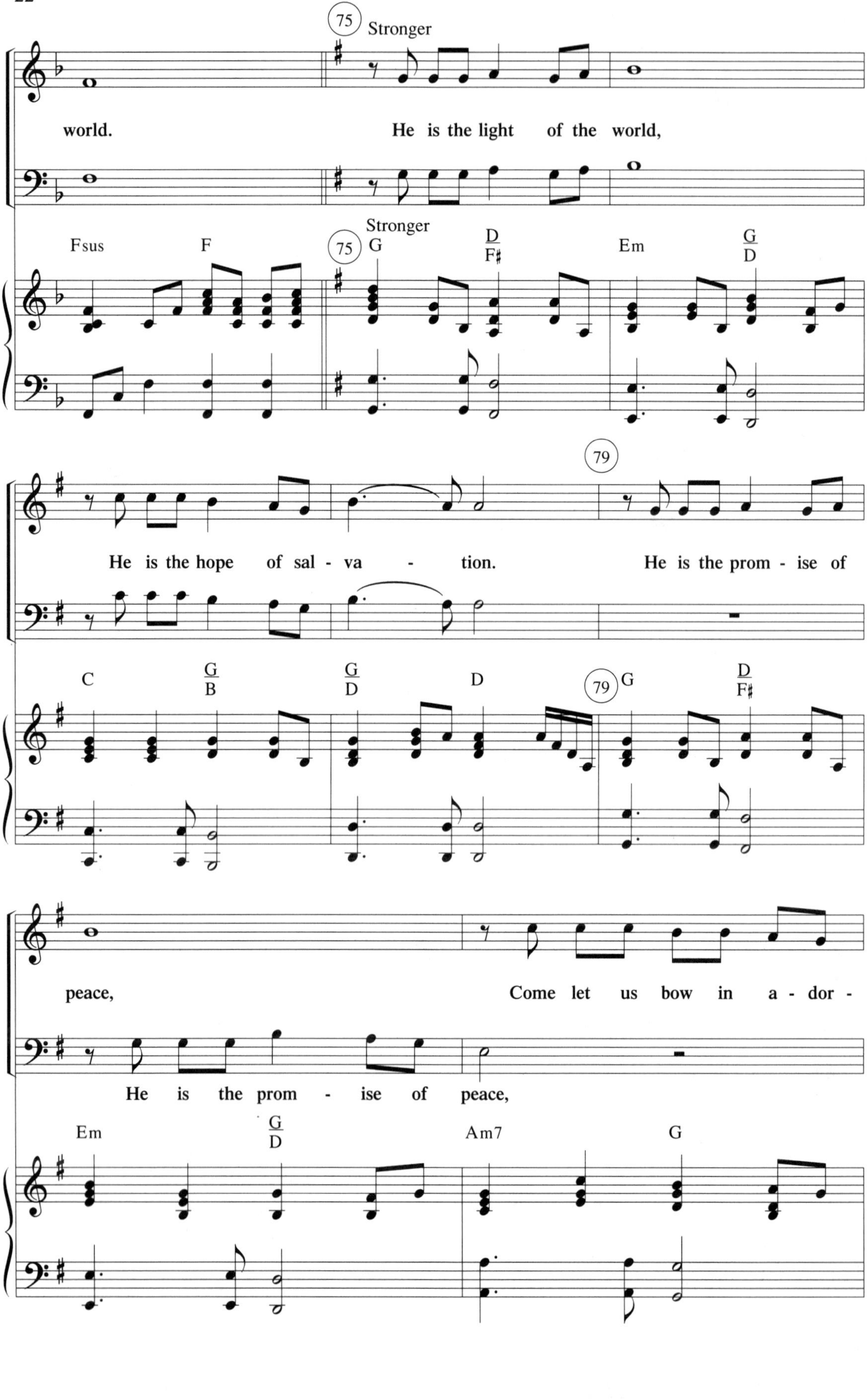
75
Stronger
world.
He is the light of the world,
Stronger
Fsus F
75 G D/F♯ Em G/D
79
He is the hope of sal - va - tion.
He is the prom - ise of
C G/B G/D D
79 G D/F♯
peace,
Come let us bow in a - dor -
He is the prom - ise of peace,
Em G/D Am7 G

25

Worship the King

B. S. and B. G.

BILLY SMILEY and BILL GEORGE
Arr. by Richard Kingsmore

Copyright © 1983 Paragon Music Corp. (ASCAP) and Yellow House Music (ASCAP).
All rights reserved. Used by permission of Benson Music Group, Inc.

VIGNETTE 1

In this scene we see an elderly grandmother in her living room where the Christmas tree is brightly decorated with presents all around. There are pictures framed everywhere. She is busy finishing preparations for a family Christmas Eve party. She is very excited, almost chatty, because this is the first time in many years that her whole family has been together at her house for Christmas. She speaks to her husband (not seen) trying to rush him along. Finally, she sits at a coffee table and thumbs through a photo album and reminisces over past Christmases and how good God has been to her.

Grandma: Hurry, Russell! The kids will be here any minute. *(looking off stage at him)* Not that tie, honey. It doesn't match your jacket. Oh, I hope that turkey isn't cooking too fast. I want everything to be just right! *(laughing)* Look at me! I'm acting like a school girl. I can't help it. It's Christmas and the whole family will be here. *(now fussing with the decorations and straightening pictures)* Johnny and the girls, well they haven't been here since the wedding and I'll bet that little Brenda is a foot taller since we last saw her. Well, I'm as ready as I can be. *(she sits down with the family photo album and sighs)* I'll just sit here and look at this photo album. Oh my, where has all the time gone? Look at those faces. Each picture a memory of Christmases long past. There's Joey! My baby is a 250 pounder, now. And Allison is just as pretty as the day I brought her home from the hospital. *(to her husband)* Do you remember that day, Russell, when Allison was born? What? No, I haven't seen your pink paisley. Why don't you wear the sweater that the kids gave you last year. And hurry! I want you out here when the kids arrive. *(back to the pictures)* Oh, my! I'd forgotten about this picture. That was the year Russell dressed up as Santa Claus. Oh, I can't wait to get my hands on the grandbaby, I'm gonna spoil him rotten. *(laughs) (music begins)* I believe I can hear the sound of every Christmas we've ever spent in this house. Oh, Lord, You've been good to me. Thank You for bringing my family home for Christmas. It's all the present I need. *(wiping a tear)* But that's just like You, Lord. You've always been faithful to me. I love You, Lord. *(reacting to a noise outside)* Russell! I think I hear the kids! *(gets up and moves off stage)* Come on, let me tie that tie for you. What would you do without me? *(exits stage holding her arms out as if to hug him)* Merry Christmas, Grandpa!

Christmas Memories (Underscore)
(Thou Didst Leave Thy Throne)

TIMOTHY R. MATTHEWS
Arr. by Richard Kingsmore

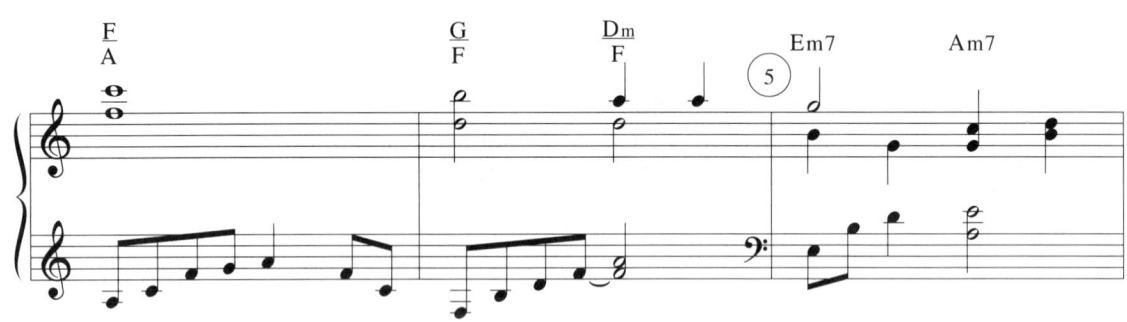

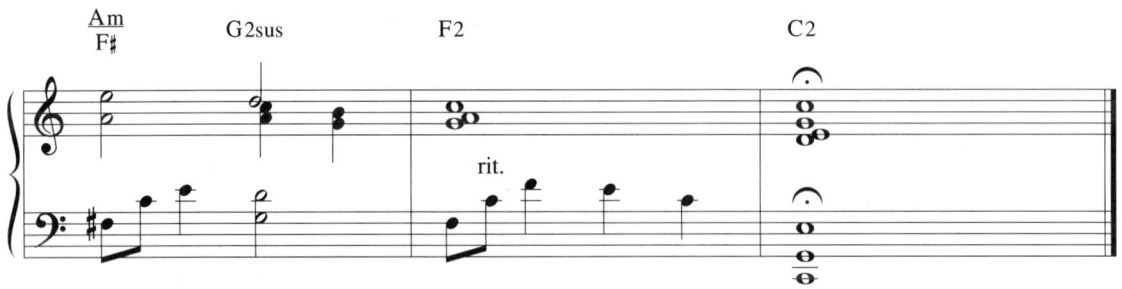

Arr. © 1996 by Pilot Point Music. All rights reserved.
Administered by The Copyright Company, 40 Music Square East, Nashville, TN 37203.

Narration 2

"Glory to God in the highest and on earth peace, good will toward men." The night the angels sang was a celebration of joy. For Jesus, the embodiment of love and joy, was born in Bethlehem of Judea. He was sent by God, the Father to care for us...and love us *(music begins)* ...and redeem us. He was sent that we might share our deepest burdens and joyfully celebrate our greatest victories with Him. He is ever-present and He is always listening with concern and compassion.

Wonderful Counselor

Words and Music by
CHRISTOPHER MACHEN
Arr. by Richard Kingsmore

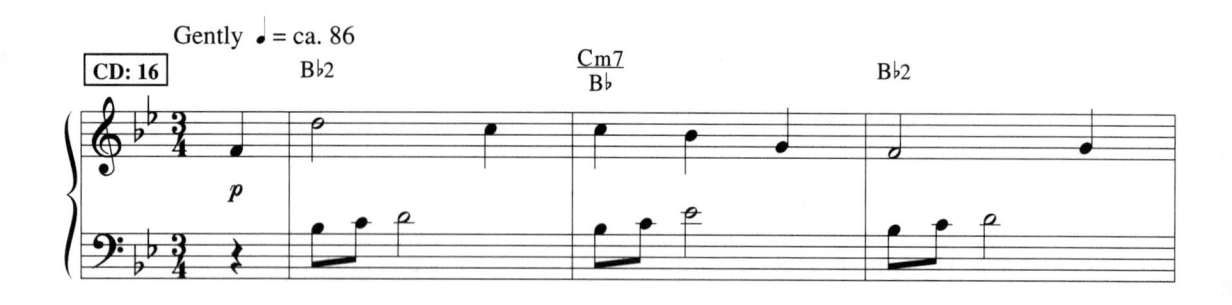

Copyright © 1996 by Pilot Point Music. All rights reserved.
Administered by The Copyright Company, 40 Music Square East, Nashville, TN 37203.

world in search of hope and love the Father heard their prayer. So the Lord in mercy sent His Son to comfort and to care.

40

CHOIR (27)

Won - der - ful Coun - sel - or,

(27) E♭ · · B♭2/D

(31) Heav - en's Love out - poured.

(31) Cm7 · F · Fm/B♭ · B♭7

(35) Won - der - ful Coun - sel - or,

(35) E♭ · · B♭/F · Gm7

41

Je - sus, the Lord.

A pre - cious gift was sent to us, The

Child was born that night. And He would be a friend to us, Our help and guiding light.

CODA

Lord. Je-sus can hear our cry; He knew sor-row, too.

Call on His wonderful name;
He came here for you.
Wonderful Counselor,

Heav - en's Love out - poured.

Won - der - ful Coun - sel - or,

Je - sus, the Lord.

97
mp
Je -
mp
G/B
Gm/B♭
97
F2
decresc.
mp
- sus, the
G2
F/G
rit.
p
Lord.
p
C
Dm/C
F/G
C2
rit.
p

VIGNETTE 2

In this scene we see a busy executive sitting at a desk, going through his mail. It's late Christmas Eve prior to the office Christmas party. He's making notes on his dictaphone when he's surprised by a letter from his wife. (Note: the letter portion can be read or at least pantomimed)

A busy man: *(looks at watch)* Okay! I'm nearly outta here! Just let me glance at this mail...probably junk...make some notes...show my face at the Christmas party... *(laughing to himself)* long enough for the boss to see me...and maybe I can get home before the kids go to bed. *(goes through the mail and makes comments to the dictaphone)* Phone bill, electric bill. Thompson and Watkins ...humph! Lawyers! Don't they know it's Christmas. Where's my dictaphone? *(to dictaphone)* Call Watkins. Oh, yeah! Remind Nelson to have that proposal to me by Monday. *(to himself)* Now, where was I? Okay, water and gas bills. What's this? *(holds letter up)* It's a letter from Karen. That's odd. Why would she write me a letter? *(opens letter, begins to read out loud)*

DEAR JERRY,
I KNOW YOU MUST BE SURPRISED TO BE GETTING A LETTER FROM ME AT YOUR OFFICE, BUT IT SEEMED TO BE THE ONLY WAY TO GET YOUR UNDIVIDED ATTENTION. YOU'RE ALWAYS TOO BUSY FOR THE BOYS AND ME. I THINK YOU LOVE YOUR JOB MORE THAN ANYTHING ...EVEN ME. YOU LEAVE BEFORE WE GET UP; YOU GET HOME WAY AFTER THE KIDS ARE IN BED. I'M SURE THEY WONDER IF THEY EVEN HAVE A FATHER. *(MUSIC BEGINS)* JERRY, IS YOUR CAREER SO IMPORTANT THAT YOU'RE WILLING TO SACRIFICE YOUR FAMILY? I LOVE YOU, HONEY, BUT WE REALLY NEED TO TALK.
        LOVE, KAREN.

(stunned, almost in tears) I didn't know...I never realized. *(trying to rationalize)* Sure, I've been a little preoccupied, but...when did my priorities get so off track? The office can survive without me...but my family desperately needs me. *(long pause, he gathers himself, straightens his tie, wipes a tear)* I've gotta call home. *(dials the phone, then breathes a prayer)* Dear God, give me the chance to make things right! *(he waits for her to answer)* Karen! It's Jerry. *(pauses)* I'm...I'm coming home, that is if you want me... *(smiles)* I love you too, Sweetheart. I'll be there in a few minutes. Merry Christmas, Honey. *(drops the phone and hurries off stage)*

The Letter (Underscore)

RICHARD KINGSMORE
Arr. by Richard Kingsmore

NARRATION 3

"In the beginning was the Word, and the Word was with God and the Word was God...All things were made by Him; and without Him was not anything made that was made." The awesome power that created the universe is available to us. Through the incarnation, God placed at man's disposal infinite resources to cope with the pressures of an earthly existence. The ultimate source of strength and power is the One who walked on water, healed the sick and raised the dead. In His strong arms, Jesus can enfold and comfort us in times of weakness and need. He can shield us from the forces which seek to rob us of a victorious life. *(music begins)* Praise God, the Father for providing Jesus Christ, our powerful Lord.

Mighty God

Words and Music by
CHRISTOPHER MACHEN
Arr. by Richard Kingsmore

There in the
When we have

si - lence of that night,
bur - dens we must bear,

Heav - en was filled with glo - rious light.
When we spend mo - ments in de - spair,

A Sav - ior was born for
Lean on the arms of

all man - kind. There is hope in Je - sus and the
faith - ful love; Rest in calm as - sur - ance know - ing

pow - er of His might.
Je - sus will be there.

He is the Might - y God,

He is the Mighty God; He is our strength when we are weak.

38
He is the Mighty - y God,
38 Em7
D/F♯
F♯
F♯/A♯
42
He is the Might - y
Bm
42 Em7
A
G/A
1 CD: 24
God.
1 Dsus
D
Dsus

55

pow - er, Je - sus, Sav - ior, Might - y God.

57

He is the Might - y God,

He is the Might - y

God; He is our strength when we are weak. He is the Mighty God,

He is the Mighty God.

He is the Mighty God,

He is the

Might - y God, Might - y God.

Prince of Peace
with
Silent Night

Words and Music by
CHRISTOPHER MACHEN
Arr. by Richard Kingsmore

All is calm, all is bright

Round yon vir - gin moth - er and Child.

Ho - ly In - fant so ten - der and mild,

25
Sleep in heav - en - ly peace,
25
E2
E7
F♯m
F♯m/E
F♯m/D♯
29
CD: 28
Sleep in heav - en - ly peace.
29
A/E
E7
A2/E
A+/E♯
33
F♯m
C♯m/E
F♯m/D♯
A2/E
Drama begins
E7sus
p
37
C♯m7/E
Bm7/E
E7
A2
rit.

Vignette 3

This scene takes place in a little girl's bedroom. She runs in, jumps on her bed, grabs a pencil paper to begin writing a special Christmas homework assignment.

Little girl: *(enters the room and jumps on the bed)* Wow! I can't believe Christmas is almost here! Only two more days and school is out for the holidays. Mrs. Ross gave us the coolest homework for tonight. All I have to do is write a paper on what I like most about Christmas. That's easy. I could fill up lots of pages about that. *(beginning to write)* I like the cold weather, and hot chocolate, and riding my bike through the leaves. I like putting up the Christmas tree, and the way the kitchen smells when Mom makes snickerdoodles. I like hearing the Christmas story at church and singing "Silent Night." I like it because the whole family is together on Christmas day and everybody laughs and tells jokes and everybody's happy. That's the best part. Everybody smiling. But I heard my Mom and Dad talking last night. Dad said he might have to take a second job because we don't have much money. He said he might have to work on Christmas day. I heard him say there won't be many presents this year. That's okay with me. I just wish he didn't have to work so hard. I miss him a lot. *(looking up from her paper)* Dear Jesus, it's me, Lindsey. I know You were a kid once, but did you ever miss Your dad? Well, I kinda have a favor to ask. This Christmas, don't worry about me. I've got plenty of good stuff. *(music begins)* But, I'd like to ask you...could Daddy be home for Christmas? That would be the best Christmas present of all.

Prince of Peace, Prince of Peace, You were

born_____ a stran - ger, You were in_____ a man - ger. Oh, come and be near_____ me, Prince of Peace._____

67

Child (or female) solo with some sopranos

Prince of Peace,

Choir with congregation

Si - lent night, ho - ly night,

Prince of Peace, You were All is calm, all is bright

born a stran - ger, You were
Round yon vir - gin moth - er and Child.

68

Sleep in heav-en-ly peace,

Sleep in heav-en-ly peace.

Silent, holy night.

rit. Choir
Ho-ly night.

Narration 4

"Behold, the virgin shall be with Child and shall bear a Son and they shall call His name Immanuel...God with us." When we are overwhelmed with fear and loneliness– He is there. When earthly relationships fail and we earnestly need the love of a father– He is there. When we cry out for help and hear nothing but silence– He is there. *(music begins)* He is Immanuel...God with us– always present, always faithful.

Everlasting Father

Words and Music by
CHRISTOPHER MACHEN
Arr. by Richard Kingsmore

72

seems. Like or-phans we've been left a-long the way. Long be-fore we had the need, God sent His Son to be The

Fa-ther who would nev-er go a-way.

Ev-er-last-ing Fa-ther, Ev-er faith-ful Friend. Heav-en's gift of love that nev-er ends. Father to the fatherless, Hope for all in hopelessness, Find in Him an everlasting Father,

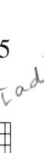

Fa - ther. In a world of shift-ing sand, With no sol-id place to stand, A heart can tum-ble down to lone-li-ness. Like a gift from heav-en's light, A Child was born that night, So we would nev-er be a-lone a-gain.

Fa-ther to the fa-ther-less, Hope for all in

77

hope - less - ness.　Find in Him　an ev - er - last - ing Fa - ther,　An ev - er - last - ing Fa - ther.

Born Is the King

including
The First Noel
Hark! the Herald Angels Sing
The Birthday of a King

With excitement ♩. = ca. 88

*"The First Noel" (Traditional English carol)

Arr. by Richard Kingsmore

Born is the King___ of___ Is - ra - el.___ The___

(Congregation optional)

---
*Arr. © 1996 by Pilot Point Music. All rights reserved. Administered by The Copyright Company, 40 Music Square East, Nashville, TN 37203.

first___ No - el, the__ an - gel did say, Was to cer - tain poor shep - herds in fields as they lay; In__ fields___ where_ they lay_ keep - ing their sheep, On a cold win-ter's night that was so deep. No-el, No-el, No-el, No-el, Born is the King of

CD: 36
37
A little faster
Is - ra - el.
C/G G7 C B♭/C C
*"Hark! the Herald Angels Sing" (Charles Wesley - Felix Mendelssohn)
39
(Cong. may continue)
Hark! the her - ald an - gels sing, "Glo - ry to the
F F/A F F/C C F/A B♭2
43
new - born King; Peace on earth, and mer - cy mild,
F/C C F C Dm Dm/C G2/B G/B

God and sin-ners rec-on-ciled!" Joy-ful, all ye na-tions rise, Join the tri-umph of the skies; With th'an-gel-ic host pro-claim, "Christ is born in

55
Beth - le - hem!" Hark! the her - ald an - gels sing,
F/C C F 55 B♭ F/A Gm D Gm
59 King."
"Glo - ry to the new - born King of
C C7/B♭ F/A Gm7 C 59 F C/F
CD: 37
61
Kings."
Al - le -
f
Majestic
B♭2/F C/E 61 D C2/D Bm/D D
f rit.

*"The Birthday of a King" (William Harold Neidlinger)

Broadly ♩ = ca. 84

lu - ia! O how the an - gels sang. Al - le - lu - ia! How it rang! And the sky was bright with a ho - ly light;

*Arr. © 1996 by Pilot Point Music. All rights reserved. Administered by The Copyright Company, 40 Music Square East, Nashville, TN 37203.

'Twas the birth-day of a King, 'Twas the birth-day of a King.

Narration 5

"For God so loved the world, that He gave His only begotten Son, that whosoever believeth in Him should not perish, but have everlasting life." In a world filled with uncertainty, God's unconditional love is absolute and unchanging. *(music begins)* He is the Wonderful Counselor, sharing our greatest joys and our deepest sorrows. He is the Mighty God, giving power and strength to those who are weak and discouraged. He is the Everlasting Father, comforting and encouraging His frightened children. He is the Prince of Peace and the Light in a world where discord and darkness prevail. He is King of Kings and Lord of Lords...Jesus– a name that is above every other name.

The Name of Jesus

with
For unto Us

Words and Music by
CHRISTOPHER MACHEN
Arr. by Richard Kingsmore

Let the name of Je-sus be praised, Let the

Copyright © 1996 by Pilot Point Music. All rights reserved.
Administered by The Copyright Company, 40 Music Square East, Nashville, TN 37203.

name of Je - sus be praised;____ For His name is a-bove all oth - er names, Let the name of Je - sus be praised. Let the name of Je - sus be praised, Let the name of Je - sus be

89

praised;   For His name is a-bove all oth-er names, Let the name of Je-sus be praised. Let the name of Je-sus be praised.

CD: 40

Faster tempo ♩ = ca. 100

*"For unto Us" (Christopher Machen)

For un-to us a Son is giv-en; For un-to us a Child is born. For un-to us a Son is giv-en, The

*Copyright © 1996 by Pilot Point Music. All rights reserved. Administered by The Copyright Company, 40 Music Square East, Nashville, TN 37203.

King of Kings and Lord of Lords. For un-to us a Son is giv-en; For un-to us a Child is born. For un-to us a Son is giv-en, The King of Kings and Lord of

Lords. He is King of Kings, He is Lord of Lords. Un-to us a Child is born!